IVOR GURNEY:

POEMS OF WAR

IVOR GURNEY: POEMS OF WAR

edited by R. K. R. Thornton

published by Rectory Press for the Ivor Gurney Society

2014

Published for
the Ivor Gurney Society
by R. K. R. Thornton at the Rectory Press
2 Rectory Terrace,
Gosforth,
Newcastle upon Tyne,
NE3 1XY
U.K.

ISBN 978-0-9572415-1-0

Preface

Noel Hayward, grandson of Ivor Gurney's sister Dorothy, is the 'onlie begetter' of this volume.

On the centenary of the outbreak of the First World War he went to the *In Flanders Fields* Museum in Ieper (the city the French call Ypres) and found that, although one of Gurney's poems had a prominent place in the exhibition, there was no small book in the shop which visitors, with little space in their luggage, could carry away to follow up an interest in Gurney's life and work.

He suggested that the Ivor Gurney Society should publish such a book and that royalties collected for use of Gurney's work could be used to help fund its publication. This book is the result of his vision, and it has received enthusiastic support from the Ivor Gurney Trust and the Ivor Gurney Society. Both those groups helped fund its production, as did Tony Boden and John Phillips, who have already done much to make Gurney better known.

Introduction

War made Ivor Gurney a poet. Until 1914 he had been concentrating on his musical development, winning a Composition scholarship to the Royal College of Music and developing his talents under Sir Charles Villiers Stanford. But the war called a halt to that, and he volunteered. Despite earlier rejections on account of his poor eyesight, he finally enlisted in the 2nd/5th Gloucester Regiment in February 1915, when the conditions of acceptance had begun to relax in the need for more and more recruits. He had written the occasional poem before then – stanzas on 'The Irish Sea' sent in 1913 to Hilaire Belloc's *The Eyewitness* (and refused) and verses for his mentor Alfred Cheesman – but the situation in the army meant that a notebook was more to hand than a piano, and his composition began to concentrate on poetry, often in friendly rivalry with his poetic friend F. W. Harvey. When he got into the trenches, the situation was even more difficult and his pencil and paper much more often – though not exclusively – used for poetry.

Readers can see, from the biographical outline which follows this introduction, where Gurney served in the war, and the various roles he took – with the water carts, machine gunner, and signaller. He wrote poetry in a constant flow wherever he was, sending back the results by the surprisingly efficient Army postal service to Marion Scott, his trusted friend and one might even say collaborator on his first book. That book, which he originally wanted to call *Songs from the Second Fifth,* was finally given the splendid title *Severn and Somme* (1917), which encapsulates the two major areas of his concern, the theatre of war into which he had been thrust and his beloved native county of Gloucestershire, with which it formed such a cruel contrast. Gloucestershire was part of Gurney's being, and he would always see the warscape in its relation to his native county, with the names and places of Gloucestershire running through his poems like a litany (see for example 'Trees' or 'That Centre of Old').

Gurney was wounded in the arm, not severely enough for it to count as a 'blighty', but he was subsequently sent home because he was gassed, just outside Ieper on hill 35, where there is now a monument in his memory.

Although returning to England meant some release from stress, his mental condition, present before the war but no doubt exacerbated by his experiences in the trenches, worsened. In the various hospitals to which he was sent, he continued to work on a second book, *War's Embers* (1919). He was discharged in October 1918, but a return to the Royal College of Music proved unsuccessful, and he failed to settle to any of the jobs he took. Confined to an asylum after 1922, he was unable to participate actively in the literary world, and the only poetry which he published after his initial two books was a handful of poems in magazines. This, and his long tedious years in the asylum, explains to some extent why his poetry took so long to emerge, although his reputation as a musician still developed, albeit slowly. Performances of his song settings were given from time to time and broadcast on the radio.

His two books, much of the material written when he was actively involved in the war, include initial enthusiasms in a Rupert Brooke-ish manner, but experience soon led him to a different view. In the immediate post-war period up to 1922, when he entered the asylum in Dartford, there was a lull in his interest in what we might generally term 'War Poetry'. But in Dartford his mind turned again to his experiences of war, this time in a more considered way. In a letter of August 3rd 1915, while writing about a Rupert Brooke sonnet, he commented that 'Great poets, great creators are not much influenced by immediate events; those must sink in to the very foundations and be absorbed'. By his asylum years, that absorption was complete. Ironically the asylum gave him the chance to write and write, alongside the need he perceived to justify himself and to hold himself together by telling again and again the story of the creative person that he had been and that he demanded that he still was.

Gurney is unlike the more famous poets of the war in several ways, which is why we have called this book *Poems of War* rather than *War Poems*. His poems do not relate to the war in quite the same way as those of his more lauded contemporaries, although in some of the notes which he wrote over and over again to establish his position among writers, he claimed the title 'first war poet'. Most important, he was not an officer nor ever anything other than a lowly and reluctant private soldier. He felt that fighting was necessary, but not something he enjoyed, though the comradeship was always a delight to him. Nor was discipline his strong point, either in verse form or in dress. In a letter of July 5th 1916 he described his relationship with his Sergeant-Major: 'When the S. M. tackled me about looking like a scarecrow – or rather ... "Come, come, Gurney, look more like a soldier for the Lord's sake." "Well, He doesn't seem to be doing much for *my* sake, and anyway I'm not a soldier. I'm a *dirty civilian*."' This laconic response to the demands of the war reflects his oblique perception of its nature.

Of equal importance are the things which Gurney chose to describe. Not for the most part the bombs and bullets, the wounds and the deaths, though he knew all about them, but the odd moments behind the lines, the simple common sense of refusing an officer's suggestion that he risk his life on the wire, the surprising pleasures to be found even amongst the gunfire, the friendships with his fellow soldiers, even curses about the weight of the books he had to carry. He mostly valued a cool, sane or cynical ability to see the whole thing askance; to take a 'stranger-view / Of life as lived in the line' as he put it in 'First Time In'. It is a point of view evident early in his writing career, as one can see in the poem, written during months of training at Seaton Delaval, 'At Reserve Depot', with its picture of the attitude of the people back in England beautifully realised in those packed lines:

The passers-by carelessly amused will see
Breakfastless boys killing the patient sack.

From this same perspective come 'The Bohemians', 'Signallers' and 'Canadians', all poems that describe the unsurprising ordinariness of soldiering that is suddenly relieved by a flash of human spirit.

We are presenting here only a selection of Gurney's poems of War, although it is impossible to say that any poem after 1914 remains untainted by its shadow. But we hope that those included will encourage readers to follow up the poetry in some of the books listed in the 'Further Reading', and perhaps also enrich their knowledge of this remarkable creative talent by exploring also some of his music.

Those who wish for a more detailed account of Gurney's writing during the war could do no better than consult the *Ivor Gurney Society Journal*, volume 19, and the essays there by Piet Chielens and Philip Lancaster.

The order of the poems is roughly, but not exactly, chronological, beginning with the poem used prominently in the *In Flanders Fields* Museum in Ieper, 'Memory let all slip', then selecting from his two published books before moving to those strange, indignant, and compelling accounts of war that he wrote in the years afterwards and in the asylum, and ending with his passionate assessment of what can be expected of poets who write of war.

R. K. R. Thornton

The focus of this edition is his poetry, but one could write an alternative biography focussing on the music, since Ivor Gurney was dually gifted. Before enlisting he had embarked upon a career to become a composer. By the outbreak of the war he had written numerous works that culminated in his *Five Elizabethan Songs* (1913/14). During his active service he was, despite the appalling conditions, able to compose a handful of songs including *By a Bierside* (1916), *Severn Meadows* (1917), *Even Such is Time,* (1917) and *In Flanders* (1917). Following his discharge from the Army in October 1918, Gurney returned to the RCM and resumed his studies, now under the tutelage of Ralph Vaughan Williams. Over the next four years Gurney composed music at an astonishing rate. These works included, a Symphony (now lost), two major orchestral essays, *A Gloucestershire Rhapsody* (1919) and *War Elegy* (1920), three string quartets, a piano trio, three violin sonatas, fifteen preludes, two sonatas for solo piano and 185 songs. Tragically, Gurney's immense creativity exacerbated his underlying illness. Indeed, the composer Gerald Finzi noted presciently something of his fragility when, after hearing a performance of Gurney's song *Sleep* in 1921, he wrote that 'one can feel the incandescence in this song that tells of something burning too brightly to last, such as you see in the filament of an electric bulb before it burns out'. During the early years of his incarceration Gurney continued to write music but as his mental decline accelerated his ability to compose tailed off and he fell silent in the late 1920s. His last song *Western Sailors* was a setting of his own words.

Ian Venables

Biographical Outline

1890   Ivor Bertie Gurney born August 28th at 3 Queen Street, Gloucester, son of David Gurney, a tailor, and his wife Florence. He had an elder sister Winifred (b.1886) and two younger siblings, Ronald (b.1894), and Dorothy (b.1900).. Alfred Cheesman, the young curate of All Saints, stood as godfather at his christening.

1890s   Family move to 19 Barton Street, a house above the shop. Attends National School and All Saints Sunday School.

1896   Purchase of family piano on which IBG learns to play.

1899   Graduates to full membership of choir of All Saints.

1900   Wins place in Gloucester Cathedral Choir, and goes to King's School. Begins to learn the organ;

1905*ff*   Years of intimacy with Cheesman, and Margaret and Emily Hunt, musicians who encourage his artistic talents.

1906   Articled pupil of Dr (later Sir) Herbert Brewer, organist of Gloucester Cathedral. Herbert Howells a fellow pupil from 1907.

1908   Meets F. W. Harvey, fellow poet and lifelong friend.

1911   Wins open composition scholarship of £40 per annum to Royal College of Music where he goes in Autumn. Cheesman provides a matching £40. Meets Marion Scott. Studies composition with Sir Charles Villiers Stanford

1912   Friendship with Herbert Howells and Arthur Benjamin. Meets Ethel Voynich.

1913   Composes the 'Elizas'. Early signs of physical and mental illness.

1914   War declared on August 4th. Gurney volunteers but is refused. Becomes organist at Christ Church, High Wycombe and becomes involved with the Chapman family.

1915   Volunteers again and enlists in the army on February 9th as Private no. 3895 of the 2nd/5th Gloucesters. Battalion goes to Northampton in February, Chelmsford in April, Epping in June, and back to Chelmsford in August. Briefly in band in September. Begins sending poems to Marion Scott. First poems published in *Royal College of Music Magazine*.

1916   To Tidworth on Salisbury Plain in February and to Park House Camp for Active Service Training. Leaves for France on May 25th. June 15th, first Front line fighting (in the Fauquissart-Laventie sector). In August in hospital for dentistry and new glasses. Plans book of poems. December to February, has job in Sanitary Section.

1917   April, wounded in upper arm on Good Friday. Sent to hospital at Rouen for six weeks. Given new number 241281 and transferred to Machine Gun Corps. Battalion moves to Ypres front in August. September 10th (?) gassed at St Julien (Passchendaele). Shipped to Bangour War Hospital in Edinburgh. Falls in love with V.A.D. nurse Annie Nelson Drummond, a relationship which does not last. *Severn & Somme* published in November. Transferred to Command Depot at Seaton Delaval.

1918 February, in Newcastle General Hospital for 'stomach trouble caused by gas'. March, convalescing at Brancepeth Castle. June, in Lord Derby's War Hospital in Warrington. July, transferred to Napsbury War Hospital, St Albans. Discharged in October with a half pension because his condition was 'aggravated but not caused by' the war. Munitions work until Armistice in November.

1919 March, second impression of *Severn & Somme*. May, death of his father. Publication of *War's Embers*. Return to Royal College of Music with Vaughan Williams as his teacher. Gurney and Harvey visit Masefield at Boar's Hill, Oxford.

1919-22 Variety of temporary jobs: organist, cinema pianist, tax officer, farm labourer. Fluent output of poems and songs. Increasing signs of mental disturbance. Formally leaves the Royal College of Music in 1921.

1922 Committed to asylum at Barnwood House in Gloucester in September and transferred to the City of London Mental Hospital at Dartford in Kent.

1923 Escapes from the asylum and visits J. C. Squire and Ralph Vaughan Williams, who informs the authorities.

1922- Much writing, some music, many poems and autobiographical-poetical letters of appeal.

1925 Is visited by Helen Thomas.

1929 Excursion to Gravesend with Marion Scott in March, who also takes him in December to see *A Midsummer Night's Dream.*

1937 Proofs of a symposium on Gurney in *Music and Letters,* containing the recognition he always craved, arrive as he is on his deathbed. Dies at Dartford on December 26th from bilateral pulmonary tuberculosis. Buried at Twigworth, near Gloucester, at the church of Alfred Cheesman.

1938 *Twenty Songs* published by Oxford University Press in two volumes.

1952 *Ivor Gurney: A Third Volume of Ten Songs* published by OUP.

1954 *Poems by Ivor Gurney: Principally selected from unpublished manuscripts* ed. Edmund Blunden, published by Heinemann.

1959 *Ivor Gurney: A Fourth Volume of Ten Songs* published by OUP.

1973 *Poems of Ivor Gurney 1890-1937* edited by Leonard Clark, published by Chatto and Windus.

1978 *The Ordeal of Ivor Gurney* by Michael Hurd published by OUP.

1982 *Collected Poems of Ivor Gurney* ed. P. J. Kavanagh published by OUP.

POEMS

Memory, Let All Slip

Memory, let all slip save what is sweet
Of Ypres plains.
Keep only autumn sunlight and the fleet
Clouds after rains,

Blue sky and mellow distance softly blue;
These only hold
Lest I my pangèd grave must share with you.
Else dead. Else cold.

To Certain Comrades
(E. S. and J. H.)

Living we loved you, yet withheld our praises
Before your faces;

And though we had your spirits high in honour,
After the English manner

We said no word. Yet, as such comrades would,
You understood.

Such friendship is not touched by Death's disaster,
But stands the faster;

And all the shocks and trials of time cannot
Shake it one jot.

Beside the fire at night some far December,
We shall remember

And tell men, unbegotten as yet, the story
Of your sad glory –

Of your plain strength, your truth of heart, your splendid
Coolness, all ended!

All ended, . . . yet the aching hearts of lovers
Joy overcovers,

Glad in their sorrow; hoping that if they must
Come to the dust,

An ending such as yours may be their portion,
And great good fortune –

That if we may not live to serve in peace
England, watching increase –

Then death with you, honoured, and swift, and high;
And so – not die.

In Trenches, July 1916

To the Poet before Battle

Now, youth, the hour of thy dread passion comes:
Thy lovely things must all be laid away;
And thou, as others, must face the riven day
Unstirred by rattle of the rolling drums,
Or bugles' strident cry. When mere noise numbs
The sense of being, the fear-sick soul doth sway,
Remember thy great craft's honour, that they may say
Nothing in shame of poets. Then the crumbs
Of praise the little versemen joyed to take
Shall be forgotten: then they must know we are,
For all our skill in words, equal in might
And strong of mettle as those we honoured; make
The name of poet terrible in just war,
And like a crown of honour upon the fight.

Maisemore

O when we swung through Maisemore,
    The Maisemore people cheered,
And women ran from farmyards,
    And men from ricks, afeared

To lose the sight of soldiers
    Who would, 'fore Christmas Day,
Blow Kaiser William's Army
    Like mist of breath away!

The war it was but young then!
    And we were young, unknowing
The path we were to tread,
    The way the path was going.

And not a man of all of us,
    Marching across the bridge,
Had thought how Home would linger
    In our hearts, as Maisemore Ridge.

When the darkness downward hovers
    Making trees like German shadows,
How our souls fly homing, homing
    Times and times to Maisemore meadows,

By Aubers ridge that Maisemore men
    Have died in vain to hold. . . .
The burning thought but once desires
    Maisemore in morning gold!

O when we marched through Maisemore
    Past many a creaking cart,
We little thought we had in us
    Love so hot at heart.

Strange Service

Little did I dream, England, that you bore me
Under the Cotswold hills beside the water meadows,
To do you dreadful service, here, beyond your borders
And your enfolding seas.

I was a dreamer ever, and bound to your dear service,
Meditating deep, I thought on your secret beauty,
As through a child's face one may see the clear spirit
Miraculously shining.

Your hills not only hills, but friends of mine and kindly,
Your tiny knolls and orchards hidden beside the river
Muddy and strongly-flowing, with shy and tiny streamlets
Safe in its bosom.

Now these are memories only, and your skies and rushy sky-pools
Fragile mirrors easily broken by moving airs. . . .
In my deep heart for ever goes on your daily being,
And uses consecrate.

Think on me too, O Mother, who wrest my soul to serve you
In strange and fearful ways beyond your encircling waters;
None but you can know my heart, its tears and sacrifice;
None, but you, repay.

To England – a Note

I watched the boys of England where they went
Through mud and water to do appointed things.
See one a stake, and one wire-netting brings,
And one comes slowly under a burden bent
Of ammunition. Though the strength be spent
They 'carry on' under the shadowing wings
Of Death the ever-present. And hark, one sings
Although no joy from the grey skies be lent.

Are these the heroes – these? have kept from you
The power of primal savagery so long?
Shall break the devil's legions? These they are
Who do in silence what they might boast to do;
In the height of battle tell the world in song
How they do hate and fear the face of War.

Ballad of the Three Spectres

As I Went up by Ovillers
    In mud and Water cold to the knee,
There went three jeering, fleering spectres,
    That walked abreast and talked of me.

The first said, 'Here's a right brave soldier
    That walks the dark unfearingly;
Soon he'll come back on a fine stretcher,
    And laughing for a nice Blighty.'

The second, 'Read his face, old comrade,
    No kind of lucky chance I see;
One day he'll freeze in mud to the marrow,
    Then look his last on Picardie.'

Though bitter the word of these first twain
    Curses the third spat venomously;
'He'll stay untouched till the war's last dawning
    Then live one hour of agony.'

Liars the first two were. Behold me
    At sloping arms by one – two – three;
Waiting the time I shall discover
    Whether the third spake verity.

Hail and Farewell

The destined bullet wounded him,
    They brought him down to die,
Far-off a bugle sounded him
    'Retreat,' Good-bye.

Strange, that from ways so hated,
    And tyranny so hard
Should come this strangely fated
    And farewell word.

He thought, 'Some Old Sweat might
    Have thrilled at heart to hear,
Gone down into the night
    Too proud to fear!

But I – the fool at arms,
    Musician, poet to boot,
Who hail release; what charms
    In this salute?'

He smiled—'The latest jest
    That time on me shall play.'
And watched the dying west,
    Went out with the day.

Trees
(*"You cannot think how ghastly these battle-fields look under a grey sky.
Torn trees are the most terrible things I have ever seen. Absolute blight
and curse is on the face of everything"*)

The dead land oppressed me;
    I turned my thoughts away,
And went where hill and meadow
    Are shadowless and gay.

Where Coopers stands by Cranham,
    Where the hill-gashes white
Show golden in the sunshine,
    Our sunshine – God's delight.

Beauty my feet stayed at last
    Where green was most cool,
Trees worthy of all worship
    I worshipped . . . then, O fool,

Let my thoughts slide unwitting
    To other, dreadful trees, . . .
And found me standing, staring
    Sick of heart – at these!

Servitude
(the third of five 'Sonnets 1917' in answer to Rupert Brooke)

If it were not for England, who would bear
This heavy servitude one moment more?
To keep a brothel, sweep and wash the floor
Of filthiest hovels were noble to compare
With this brass-cleaning life. Now here, now there
Harried in foolishness, scanned curiously o'er
By fools made brazen by conceit, and store
Of antique witticisms thin and bare.

Only the love of comrades sweetens all,
Whose laughing spirit will not be outdone.
As night-watching men wait for the sun
To hearten them, so wait I on such boys
As neither brass nor Hell-fire may appal,
Nor guns, nor sergeant-major's bluster and noise.

'Wind from the sea, roaming desolate places'

Wind from the sea, roaming desolate places
Scarred by the spade, footprint and burst of shell –
You bring us here thoughts of long dreamt on faces,
Hedges of spring foam edged like the near-beach swell,
And tears at heart, for joy by Fate denied
So long, that hope itself had almost died.
In broken woods of horror the sweet breeze drifts
And stirs the tattered leafage with tender soft
Touches of love, whereat the smoke cloud lifts,
Hovers, and disappears, wandering aloft.

The wind of home smooths
War from the new-clean air.

Camps

Out of the line we rest in villages
    Quiet indeed, where heal the spirit's scars;
But even so, lapped deep in sunshine and ease,
    We are haunted for ever by the shapes of wars.

Green in the sun they lie, secret, deserted,
    Lovely against the blue the summits show,
Where once the bright steel sang, the red blood spurted
    And brave men cowed their terrors long ago.

By day their life was easy; but at night,
    Even now, one hears strange rustlings in the bush;
And, straining tensely doubtful ear and sight,
    The stealthy moving ere the sudden rush;

And flinches from the spear. War's just-bright embers
    That Earth still keeps and treasures for the pride
In sacrifice there shown; with love remembers
    The beauty and quick strength of men that died.

Who died as we may die, for Freedom, beauty
    Of common living, calmly led in peace,
Yet took the flinty road and hard of duty,
    Whose end was life abundant and increase.

But – when Heaven's gate wide opening receives us
    Victors and full of song, forgetting scars;
Shall we see to stir old memories, to grieve us,
    Heaven's never-yet-healed sores of Michael's wars?

At Reserve Depot

When Spring comes here with early innocency
    Of pale high blue, they'll put Revally back.
The passers-by carelessly amused will see
    Breakfastless boys killing the patient sack.

And there will be manoeuvres where the violet shows,
    Hiding its dark fervour, guarding its flame,
Where I shall lie and stare while the mystery grows
    Huge and more huge, till the Sergeant calls my name.

Toasts and Memories
(To the Men of the 2/5 Gloucester Regiment)

When once I sat in estaminets
    With trusty friends of mine,
We drank to folk in England
    And pledged them well in wine,

While thoughts of Gloucester filled us –
    Roads against windy skies
At sunset, Severn river,
    Red inn-blinds, country cries,

That stung the heart with sorrow
    And barbéd sweet delight
At Riez Bailleul, Laventie,
    At Merville, many a night.

Now I am over Channel
    I cannot help but think
Of friends who stifle longing
    With friendly food and drink.

'Where's Gurney now, I wonder,
    That smoked a pipe all day;
Sometimes that talked like blazes,
    Sometimes had naught to say?'

And I, at home, must wonder
    Where all my comrades are:
Those men whose Heart-of-Beauty
    Was never stained by War.

To his Love

He's gone, and all our plans
    Are useless indeed.
We'll walk no more on Cotswold
    Where the sheep feed
    Quietly and take no heed.

His body that was so quick
    Is not as you
Knew it, on Severn river
    Under the blue
    Driving our small boat through.

You would not know him now . . .
    But still he died
Nobly, so cover him over
    With violets of pride
    Purple from Severn side.

Cover him, cover him soon!
    And with thick-set
Masses of memoried flowers –
    Hide that red wet
    Thing I must somehow forget.

The Target

I shot him, and it had to be
One of us! 'Twas him or me.
'Couldn't be helped,' and none can blame
Me, for you would do the same.

My mother, she can't sleep for fear
Of what might be a-happening here
To me. Perhaps it might be best
To die, and set her fears at rest.

For worst is worst, and worry's done.
Perhaps he was the only son . . .
Yet God keeps still, and does not say
A word of guidance any way.

Well, if they get me, first I'll find
That boy, and tell him all my mind,
And see who felt the bullet worst,
And ask his pardon, if I durst.

All's a tangle. Here's my job.
A man might rave, or shout, or sob;
And God He takes no sort of heed.
This is a bloody mess indeed.

Recompense
(To the Men of the 2/5 Gloucester Regiment)

I'd not have missed one single scrap of pain
That brought me to such friends, and them to me;
And precious is the smallest agony,
The greatest, willingly to bear again –
Cruel frost, night vigils, death so often ta'en
By Golgothas untold from Somme to Sea.
Duty's a grey thing; Friendship valorously
Rides high above all Fortune without stain.

Their eyes were stars within the blackest night
Of Evil's trial. Never mariner
Did trust so in the ever-fixéd star
As I in those. And so their laughter sounded –
Trumpets of Victory glittering in sunlight;
Though Hell's power ringed them in, and night surrounded.

'On Rest'
(To the Men of the 2/5 Gloucester Regiment)

It's a King's life, a life for a King!
To lie safe sheltered in some old hay-loft
Night long, on golden straw, and warm and soft,
Unroused; to hear through dreams dawn's thrushes sing
'Revally' – drowse again; then wake to find
The bright sun through the broken tiles thick-streaming
'Revally' real: and there's an end to dreaming.
'Up, Boys, and Out!' Then O what green, what still
Peace in the orchard, deep and sweet and kind,
Shattered abruptly – splashing water, shout
On shout of sport, and cookhouse vessels banging,
Dixie against dixie musically clanging. –
The farmer's wife, searching for eggs, 'midst all
Dear farmhouse cries. A stroll: and then 'Breakfast's up.'
Porridge and bacon! Tea out of a real cup
(Borrowed). First day on Rest, a Festival
Of mirth, laughter in safety, a still air.
'No whizzbangs,' 'crumps' to fear, nothing to mind,
Danger and the thick brown mud behind,
An end to wiring, digging, end to care.
Now wonders begin, Sergeants with the crowd
Mix; Corporals, Lance-Corporals, little proud,
Authority forgotten, all goes well
In this our Commonwealth, with tales to tell,
Smokes to exchange, letters of price to read,
Letters of friends more sweet than daily bread.
The Sergeant-major sheathes his claws and lies
Smoking at length, content deep in his eyes.
Officers like brothers chaff and smile –
Salutes forgotten, etiquette the while,
Comrades and brothers all, one friendly band.
Now through the orchard (sun-dried of dewfall) in
And out the trees the noisy sports begin.
He that is proud of body runs, leaps, turns
Somersaults, hand-turns; the licensed jester flings
Javelins of blunt wit may bruise not pierce;

Ragtimes and any scrap of nonsense sings.
All's equal now. It's Rest, none cares, none escapes
The hurtless battering of those kindly japes.
Noon comes, the estaminets open welcome doors,
Men drift along the roads in three and fours,
Enter those cool-paven rooms, and sit
Waiting; many there are to serve, Madame
Forces her way with glasses, all ignores
The impatient clamour of that thirsty jam,
The outcries, catcalls, queries, doubtful wit,
Alike. Newspapers come, 'Journal, m'sieur?'
'What's the news?' 'Anything fresh, boy?' 'Tell us what's new.'
Dinner, perhaps a snooze, perhaps a stroll.
Tea, letters (most like), rations to divide
(Third of a loaf, half, if luck's our way).
No work, no work, no work! A lovely day!
Down the main street men loiter side by side.
So day goes on blue-domed till the west's afire
With the sun just sunken, though we cannot see,
Hidden in green, the fall of majesty.
Our hearts are lifted up, fierce with desire
But once again to see the ricks, the farms,
Blue roads, still trees of home in the rich glow;
Life's pageant fading slower and more slow
Till Peace folds all things in with tender arms.
The last stroll in the orchard ends, the last
Candles are lit in bivvy and barn and cart,
Where comrades talking lie, comfort at heart,
Gladder for danger shared in the hard past,
The stars grow bright 'gainst heaven's still-deepening blue,
Lights in the orchard die. 'I wonder how
Mother is keeping: she must be sleepy now
As we, yet may be wondering all night through.'

Dicky
(To His Memory)

They found him when the day
Was yet but gloom;
Six feet of scarréd clay
Was ample room
And wide enough domain for all desires
For him, whose glowing eyes
Made mock at lethargies,
Were not a moment still; –
Can Death, all slayer, kill
The fervent source of those exultant fires?
Nay, not so;
Somewhere that glow
And starry shine so clear astonishes yet
The wondering spirits as they come and go.
Eyes that nor they nor we shall ever forget.

Omiecourt

Le Coq Français

After the biting cold of the outer night
It seemed – ('Le Coq Français') – a palace of light,
And its low roof black-timbered was most fine
After the iron and sandbags of the line.
Easy it was to be happy there! Madame,
Frying a savoury mess of eggs and ham,
Talking the while: of the War, of the crops, her son
Who should see to them, and would, when the War was done.
Of battalions who had passed there, happy as we
To find a house so clean, such courtesy
Simple, sincere; after vigils of frost
The place seemed the seventh Heaven of comfort; lost
In miraculous strange peace and warmth we'd sit
Till the prowling police hunted us out of it –
Away from café noir, café au lait, vin blanc,
Vin rouge, citron, all that does belong
To the kindly shelter of old estaminets,
Nooked and cornered, with mirth of firelight ablaze –
Herded us into billets; where candles must show
Little enough comfort after the steady glow
Of that wonderful fireshine. We must huddle us close
In blankets, hiding all but the crimson nose,
To think awhile of home, if the frost would let
Thought flow at all; then sleep, sleep to forget
All but home and old rambles, lovely days
Of maiden April, glamorous September haze,
All darling things of life, the sweet of desire –
Castles of Spain in the deep heart of the fire.

'Annie Laurie'

The high barn's lit by many a guttering flare
    Of flickering candle, dangerous – (hence forbidden) –
    To warm soft straw, whereby the cold floor's hidden
On which we soon shall rest without a care.
War is forgotten. Gossip fills the air
    Of home, and laughter sounds beyond the midden
    Under the stars, where Youth makes Joy unchidden
Of gods or men, and mocks at sorrow there.
But hark! what sudden pure untainted passion
    Seizes us now, and stills the garrulous?
A song of old immortal dedication
      To Beauty's service and one woman's heart.
    No tears we show, no sign of flame in us
      This hour of stars and music set apart.

Photographs
(To Two Scots Lads)

Lying in dug-outs, joking idly, wearily;
    Watching the candle guttering in the draught;
Hearing the great shells go high over us, eerily
    Singing; how often have I turned over, and laughed

With pity and pride, photographs of all colours,
    All sizes, subjects: khaki brothers in France;
Or mother's faces worn with countless dolours;
    Or girls whose eyes were challenging and must dance,

Though in a picture only, a common cheap
    Ill-taken card; and children – frozen, some
(Babies) waiting on Dicky-bird to peep
    Out of the handkerchief that is his home

(But he's so shy!). And some with bright looks, calling
    Delight across the miles of land and sea,
That not the dread of barrage suddenly falling
    Could quite blot out – not mud nor lethargy.

Smiles and triumphant careless laughter. O
    The pain of them, wide Earth's most sacred things!
Lying in dugouts, hearing the great shells slow
    Sailing mile-high, the heart mounts higher and sings.

But once – O why did he keep that bitter token
    Of a dead Love? – that boy, who, suddenly moved,
Showed me, his eyes wet, his low talk broken,
    A girl who better had not been beloved.

First March

It was first marching, hardly we had settled yet
To think of England, or escaped body pain –
Flat country going leaves but small chance for
The mind to escape to any resort but its vain
Own circling greyness and stain.
First halt, second halt, and then to the spoiled country again
There were unknown kilometres to march, one must settle
To play chess or talk hometalk or think as might happen.
After three weeks of February frost few were in fettle,
Barely frostbite the most of us had escapen.
To move, then to go onward, at last to be moved.
Myself had revived and then dulled down, it was I
Who stared for body-ease at the grey sky
And watched in grind of pain the monotony
Of grit road metal slide underneath by.
To get there being the one way not to die.
Suddenly a road's turn brought the sweet unexpected
Balm. Snowdrops bloomed in a ruined garden neglected:
Roman the road as Birdlip, we were on the verge,
And this west country thing so from chaos to emerge.
One gracious touch the whole wilderness corrected.

Laventie

One would remember still
Meadows and low hill
Laventie was, as to the line and elm row
Growing through green strength wounded, as home elms grow.
Shimmer of summer there and blue autumn mists
Seen from trench-ditch winding in mazy twists.
The Australian gunners in close flowery hiding
Cunning found out at last, and smashed in the unspeakable lists
And the guns in the smashed wood thumping and griding.
The letters written there, and received there,
Books, cakes, cigarettes in a parish of famine,
And leaks in rainy times with general all-damning.
The crater, and carrying of gas cylinders on two sticks
(Pain past comparison and far past right agony gone),
Strained hopelessly of heart and frame at first fix.

Café-au-lait in dug-outs on Tommies' cookers,
Cursed minniewerfs, thirst in eighteen-hour summer.
The Australian miners clayed, and the being afraid
Before strafes, sultry August dusk time than death dumber –
And the cooler hush after the strafe, and the long night wait –
The relief of first dawn, the crawling out to look at it,
Wonder divine of dawn, man hesitating before Heaven's gate.
(Though not on Cooper's where music fire took at it.
Though not as at Framilode beauty where body did shake at it)
Yet the dawn with aeroplanes crawling high at Heaven's gate
Lovely aerial beetles of wonderful scintillate
Strangest interest, and puffs of soft purest white –
Seeking light, dispersing colouring for fancy's delight.
Of Machonachie, Paxton, Tickler and Gloucester's Stephens;
Fray Bentos, Spiller and Baker, odds and evens
Of trench food, but the everlasting clean craving
For bread, the pure thing, blessèd beyond saving.
Canteen disappointments, and the keen boy braving
Bullets or such for grouse roused surprisingly through
(Halfway) Stand-to.
And the shell nearly blunted my razor at shaving;

Tilleloy, Fauquissart, Neuve Chapelle, and mud like glue.
But Laventie, most of all, I think is to soldiers
The town itself with plane trees, and small-spa air;
And vin, rouge-blanc, chocolat, citron, grenadine:
One might buy in small delectable cafés there.
The broken church, and vegetable fields bare;
Neat French market-town look so clean,
And the clarity, amiability of North French air.
                          *
Like water flowing beneath the dark plough and high Heaven,
Music's delight to please the poet pack-marching there.

That Centre of Old

Is it only Cotswold that holds the glamour
Memory felt of England in the gun-stammer –
Thud, smack, belch of war – and kept virtue by?
I do not know, but only that, most unhappy,
The hills are to me what to happy I
They were in Somme muckage-baths and east of Laventie
When hunger made one worthy to absorb the sky –
Look, or play fancy-tricks with small cloudlets high:
Count them – or dare not count – love and let go by.
Now as ever Cotswold rewards the mere being and seeing
As truly as
Ever in the relief of knowing mere being
In the still space
At a strafe end grateful for silence and body's grace
(Whole body – and after hell's hammering and clamouring.)
Then memory purified made rewarding shapes
Of all that spirit runs towards in escapes,
And Cooper's Hill showed plain almost as experience.
Soft winter mornings of kind innocence, high June's
Girl's air of untouched purity and on Cooper's Hill
Or Autumn Cranham with its boom of colour . . .
Not anyway does ever Cotswold's fail – Her dear blue long
                              dark slope fail – '
Of the imagining promise in full exile.

New Year's Eve

Aveluy and New Year's Eve, and the time as tender
As if green buds grew. In the low west a slender
Streak of last orange. Guns mostly deadest still.
And a noise of limbers near coming down the hill.
Nothing doing, nothing doing, and a screed to write,
Candles enough for books, a sleepy delight
In the warm dug-out, day ended. Nine hours to the light.
There now and then now, one nestled down snug.
A head is enough to read by, and cover up with a rug.
Electric. Clarinet sang of 'A Hundred Pipers'
And hush awe mystery vanished like tapers
Of tobacco smoke, there was great hilarity then!
Breath, and a queer tube, magicked sorrow from men.
The North, and all Scott called me – Ballads and Burns again!
Enough! I got up and lit (the last little bit
But one) of candle and poked the remaining fire,
Got some blaze into the cold; sat, wrote verse there . . .
(Or music). The 'hundred pipers' had called so plain
('And a') and for three hours stuck it and worked as best
Drippings, and cold, and misery would let desire.

Crucifix Corner

There was a water dump there and regimental
Carts came every day to line up and fill full
Those rolling tanks with chlorinated clay mixture
And curse the mud with vain veritable vexture.
Aveluy across the valley, billets, shacks, ruins.
With time and time a crump there to mark doings.
On New Year's Eve the marsh gloomed tremulous
With rosy mist still holding so marvellous
Sunglow; the air smelt home; the time breathed home –
Noel not put away; New Year's Eve not yet come.
All things said 'Severn', the air was of those dusk meadows –
Transport rattled somewhere in southern shadows,
Stars that were not strange ruled the lit tranquil sky,
Arched far and high.

What should break that but gun-noise or last Trump?
Neither broke it. Suddenly at a light jump
Clarinet sang into 'Hundred Pipers and a'
Aveluy's pipers answered with pipers' true call
'Happy we've been a'-tegether' when nothing, nothing
Stayed of war-weariness or winter-loathing.
Cracker with stockings hung in the quaint Heavens
Orion and the seven stars comical at odds and evens -
Gaiety split discipline in sixes or sevens –
Hunger mixed strangely with magical leavens.
It was as if Cinderella had opened the Ball
And music put aside the time's saddened clothing.
It was as if Sir Walter were company again
In the late night – *Antiquary* or *Midlothian* –
Or *Redgauntlet* bringing Solway clear to the mind.
After music, and a day of walking or making
To return to music, or to read the starred dark dawn-blind.

Near Vermand

Lying flat on my belly shivering in clutch-frost,
There was time to watch the stars, we had dug in:
Looking eastward over the low ridge; March scurried its blast
At our senses, no use either dying or struggling.
Low woods to left – (Cotswold her spinnies if ever)
Showed through snow flurries and the clearer star weather,
And nothing but chill and wonder lived in mind; nothing
But loathing and fine beauty, and wet loathed clothing.
Here were thoughts. Cold smothering and fire-desiring,
A day to follow like this or in the digging or wiring.
                    *
Worry in snow flurry and lying flat, flesh the earth loathing.
I was the forward sentry and would be relieved
In a quarter or so, but nothing more better than to crouch
Low in the scraped holes and to have frozen and rocky couch –
To be by desperate home thoughts clutched at, and heart-grieved
Was I ever there – a lit warm room and Bach, to search out sacred
Meaning; and to find no luck; and to take love as believed?

First Time In

The Captain addressed us; Afterglow grew deeper,
Like England, like the west country, and stars grew thicker.
In silence we left the billet, we found the hard roadway
In single file, jangling (silent) and on the grey
Chipped road, moaned over ever by snipers' shots.
Got shelter in the first trench; and the thud of boots
On duck-board wood from grate on rough road stone it changed
(Very lights showed ghastly, and a machine-gun ranged.)
Sentry here and there. How the trench wound now! Wires
Hindered, thistles pricked, but few guns spat their fires.
Upward a little . . . wider a little, the reserve line reached.
Tin hat shapes, dark body shapes and faces as bleached.
And the heart's beat: 'Here men are maimed and shot through,
                              hit through;
Here iron and lead rain, sandbags rent in two;
And the honours are earned. The stuff of tales is woven.
Here were whispers of encouragement, about the cloven
Trenches faces showed and west soft somethings were said.
Lucky were signallers who (intellectual) strangely had
Some local independence in line danger, but
In training or on Rest were from honour shut.
Bundling over sky lines to clear trench digging –
On the Plain scorn went with tapping and flag wagging
Directions. And then one took us courteously
Where a sheet lifted, and gold light cautiously
Streamed from an oilsheet slitted vertical into
Half-light of May. We entered, took stranger-view
Of life as lived in the line, the line of war and daily
Papers, despatches, brave-soldier talks, the really, really
Truly line, and these the heroes of story.

Never were quieter folk in teaparty history.
Never in *Cranford*, Trollope, even. And, as it were, home.
Closed round us. They told us lore, how and when did come
Minnewerfers and grenades from over there east;
The pleasant and unpleasant habits of the beast
That crafted and tore Europe. What line-mending was

41

When guns centred and dug-outs rocked in a haze
And hearing was difficult – (wires cut) – all necessary
Common-sense workmanlike cautions of salutary
Wisdom – the mechanic day-lore of modern war-making,
Calm thought discovered in mind and body shaking.
The whole craft and business of bad occasion.
Talk turned personal, and to borders of two nations
Gone out; Cotswold's Black Mountain edges against august
August after-sun's glow, and air a lit dust
With motes and streams of gold. Wales her soul visible
Against all power west Heaven ever could flood full.
And of songs – the 'Slumber Song', and the soft Chant
So beautiful to which Rabelaisian songs were meant
Of South and North Wales; and 'David of the White Rock':
What an evening! What a first time, what a shock
So rare of home-pleasure beyond measure
And always to time's ending surely a treasure.

*

Since after-war so surely hurt, disappointed men
Who looked for the golden Age to come friendly again.
With inn evenings of meetings in warm glows,
Talk: coal and wood fire uttering rosy shows
With beer and 'Widdicombe Fair' and five mile homeward —
Moonlight lying thick on frost spangled fleet foot sward,
And owl crying out every short while his one evil word.

At any rate, disputeless the romantic evening was –
The night, the midnight; next day Fritz strafed at us,
And I lay belly upward to wonder: when – but useless.

Canadians

We marched, and saw a company of Canadians,
Their coats weighed eighty pounds at least, we saw them
Faces infinitely grimed in, with almost dead hands
Bent, slouching downwards to billets comfortless and dim.
Cave dwellers last of tribes they seemed, and a pity
Even from us just relieved, much as they were, left us.
Lord, what a land of desolation, what iniquity
Of mere being, of what youth that country bereft us;
Plagues of evil lay in Death's Valley, we also
Had forded that up to the thighs in chill mud,
Gone for five days then any sign of life glow,
As the notched stumps or the grey clouds we stood
Dead past death from first hour and the needed mood
Of level pain shifting continually to and fro.
Saskatchewan, Ontario, Jack London ran in
My own mind; what in others? these men who finely
Perhaps had chosen danger for reckless and fine,
Fate had sent for suffering and dwelling obscenely
Vermin-eaten, fed beastly, in vile ditches meanly.

Of Grandcourt

Through miles of mud we travelled, and by sick valleys –
The Valley of Death at last – most evil alleys,
To Grandcourt trenches reserve – and the hell's name it did deserve.
Rain there was – tired and weak I was, glad for an end.
But one spoke to me – one I liked well as friend,
'Let's volunteer for the Front Line – many others won't.
I'll volunteer, it's better being there than here.'
But I had seen too many ditches and stood too long
Feeling my feet freeze, and my shoulders ache with the strong
Pull of equipment, and too much use of pain and strain.
Beside, he was Lance Corporal and might be full Corporal
Before the next straw resting might come again,
Before the next billet should hum with talk and song.
Stars looked as well from second as from first line holes.
There were fatigues for change, and a thought less danger –
But five or six there were followed Army with their souls
Took five days dripping rain without let or finish again –
With dysentery and bodies of heroic ghouls.
Till at last their hearts feared nothing of the brazen anger,
(Perhaps of death little) but once more again to drop on straw
                                    bed-serving,
And to have heaven of dry feeling after the damps and fouls.

The Silent One

Who died on the wires, and hung there, one of two –
Who for his hours of life had chartered through
Infinite lovely chatter of Bucks accent:
Yet faced unbroken wires; stepped over, and went
A noble fool, faithful to his stripes – and ended.
But I weak, hungry, and willing only for the chance
Of line – to fight in the line, lay down under unbroken
Wires, and saw the flashes and kept unshaken,
Till the politest voice – a finicking accent, said:
'Do you think you might crawl through there: there's a hole.'
Darkness, shot at: I smiled, as politely replied –
'I'm afraid not, Sir.' There was no hole no way to be seen
Nothing but chance of death, after tearing of clothes.
Kept flat, and watched the darkness, hearing bullets whizzing –
And thought of music – and swore deep heart's deep oaths
(Polite to God) and retreated and came on again,
Again retreated – and a second time faced the screen.

Strange Hells

There are strange hells within the minds war made
Not so often, not so humiliatingly afraid
As one would have expected – the racket and fear guns made
One hell the Gloucester soldiers they quite put out:
Their first bombardment, when in combined black shout
Of fury, guns aligned, they ducked lower their heads
And sang with diaphragms fixed beyond all dreads,
That tin and stretched-wire tinkle, that blither of tune:
'Après la guerre fini', till hell all had come down,
Twelve-inch, six-inch, and eighteen pounders hammering hell's
thunders.

Where are they now, on state-doles, or showing shop-patterns
Or walking town to town sore in borrowed tatterns
Or begged. Some civic routine one never learns.
The heart burns – but has to keep out of face how heart burns

Riez Bailleul

Behind the line there mending reserve posts, looking
On the cabbage fields with other men carefully tending cooking;
Hearing the boiling; and being sick of body and heart,
Too sick for anything but hoping that all might depart –
We back in England again, and white roads to walk on,
Eastwards to hill-steeps, or see meadows good to talk on.
Grey Flanders sky over all and a heaviness felt
On the sense that no working or dreaming would any way melt . . .
This is not happy thought, but a glimpse most strangely
Forced from the past, to hide this pain and work myself free
From present things. The parapet, the grey look-out, the making
Of a peasantry, by dread war, harried and set on shaking;
A hundred things of age, and of carefulness,
Spoiling; a farmer's treasure perhaps soon a wilderness.

On Somme

Suddenly into the still air burst thudding
And thudding, and cold fear possessed me all,
On, the grey slopes there, where winter in sullen brooding
Hung between height and depth of the ugly fall
Of Heaven to earth; and the thudding was illness' own.
But still a hope I kept that were we there going over,
I in the line, I should not fail, but take recover
From others' courage, and not as coward be known.
No flame we saw, the noise and the dread alone
Was battle to us; men were enduring there such
And such things, in wire tangled, to shatters blown.

Courage kept, but ready to vanish at first touch.
Fear, but just held. Poets were luckier once
In the hot fray swallowed and some magnificence.

While I Write

While l write war tells me truth; as for brave
None might challenge Gloucesters, save those dead who have
Paid prices for pre-eminence, perhaps have got their pay.
But the common goodness of those soldiers shown day after day
And the sight of each-hour beauty brilliant or most grave,
Stays with me yet. While I am forbidden to write
Tale of the continual readiness for a bad bloodiness,
And steadiness against hell-fire; and strained eyes with humour bright.
War told me truth: I have Severn's right of maker,
As of Cotswold: war told me: I was elect, l was born fit
To praise the three hundred feet depth of every acre
Between Tewkesbury and Stroudway, Side and Wales Gate.

It Is Near Toussaints

It is near Toussaints, the living and dead will say:
'Have they ended it? What has happened to Gumey?'
And along the leaf-strewed roads of France many brown shades
Will go, recalling singing, and a comrade for whom also they
Had hoped well. His honour them had happier made.
Curse all that hates good. When I spoke of my breaking
(Not understood) in London, they imagined of the taking
Vengeance, and seeing things were different in future.
(A musician was a cheap, honourable and nice creature.)
Kept sympathetic silence; heard their packs creaking
And burst into song – Hilaire Belloc was all our master.
On the night of all the dead, they will remember me,
Pray Michael, Nicholas, Maries lost in Novembery
River-mist in the old City of our dear love, and batter
At doors about the farms crying 'Our war poet is lost.
Madame – no bon!' – and cry his two names, warningly, sombrely.

The Battle

The Gloucesters were to go over I was not one –
Glad because of the terribleness, ashamed because of the terror,
I saw in the loveliest azure mist September had shown
Great spouts of white, heard thunders and knew that somewhere
Gloucesters were moving, men for three years I had known
Perhaps to see no more – fallen from thought of their shire
Even. High over all, guard on a machine-gun
Which yet might be needed (doubt at Ypres the surer)
I saw blue mist and white smoke, but never fire,
Who heard two days after such names I had sworn
Had long ago saved me – of men fallen by battle torn,
Whether alive or dead – I had sworn to their power.

Serenade

It was after the Somme, our line was quieter,
Wires mended, neither side daring attacker
Or aggressor to be – the guns equal, the wires a thick hedge,
When there sounded, (O past days for every confounded!)
The tune of Schubert which belonged to days mathematical,
Effort of spirit bearing fruit worthy, actual.
The gramophone for an hour was my quiet's mocker,
Until I cried, 'Give us "Heldenleben", "Heldenleben".'
The Gloucesters cried out 'Strauss is our favourite wir haben
Sich geliebt'. So silence fell, Aubers front slept,
And the sentries an unsentimental silence kept.
True, the size of the rum ration was still a shocker
But at last over Aubers the majesty of the dawn's veil swept.

The Bohemians

Certain people would not clean their buttons,
Nor polish buckles after latest fashions,
Preferred their hair long, putties comfortable,
Barely escaping hanging, indeed hardly able;
In Bridge and smoking without army cautions
Spending hours that sped like evil for quickness,
(While others burnished brasses, earned promotions).
These were those ones who jested in the trench,
While others argued of army ways, and wrenched
What little soul they had still further from shape,
And died off one by one, or became officers.
Without the first of dream, the ghost of notions
Of ever becoming soldiers, or smart and neat,
Surprised as ever to find the army capable
Of sounding 'Lights out' to break a game of Bridge,
As to fear candles would set a barn alight:
In Artois or Picardy they lie – free of useless fashions.

Signallers

To be signallers and to be relieved two hours
Before the common infantry – and to come down
Hurriedly to where estaminet's friendliest doors
Opened – where before the vulgar brawling common crew
Could take the seats for tired backs, or take the wine
Best suited for palates searching for delicate flavours
(Or pretty tints) to take from the mind trench ways and the strain,
Though it be on tick, with delicately wangled sly favours.
Then having obtained grace from the lady of the inn –
How good to sit still and sip with all-appreciative lip,
(After the grease and skilly of line-cookhouse tea)
The cool darkling texture of the heavenly dew
Of wine – to smoke as one pleased in a house of courtesy –
Signallers, gentlemen, all away from the vulgar
Infantry – so dull and dirty and so underpaid,
So wont to get killed and leave the cautious signallers
To signal down the message that they were dead.
Anyway, distinctions or not – there was a quiet
Hour or so before the Company fours halted, and were
Formed two-deep, and dismissed and paid after leaden, dilatory
Hanging around, to bolt (eager) to find those apparently
Innocent signallers drinking, on tick, at last beer.

Varennes

At Varennes also Gloucester men had their stay.
(Infantry again, of my soft job getting tired.)
Saw wonderful things of full day and of half-day:
Black pattern of twigs against the sunset dim fired;
Stars like quick inspirations of God in the seven o'clock sky
Where the infantry drilled frozen – all all foolishly
As on the Plain – but to the canteen went I,
Got there by high favour, having run, finished third,
In a mile race from Varennes to the next village end.
Canteen assistant, with a special care for B Company –
And biscuits hidden for favour in a manner forbidden.
Lying about chocolate to C Company hammering the gate.
Pitying them for their parades all the morning through
(Blue to the fingers, to all but the conscience blue)
Uselessly doing fatheaded things eternally.
But keeping (as was natural) Six Platoon ever in mind.
And one evening, drowsed by the wood fire I got lost in the
Blaze of warm embers, green wood smoking annoyingly;
Watched deep till my soul in the magic was rapt asleep:
Grew to power of music, and all poetries, so, uncared,
Became a maker among soldiers – dear comrades;
Which is the hardest of all wide earth's many trades;
And so proved my birthright, in a minute of warm aired
Staring into the woodfire's poetic heart, lost a tide deep.
(Until the anger of fire caught all, all in rose or gold was lost)

Portrait of a Coward

True he'd have fought to death if the Germans came –
But an hour's battering after a day's battering
Brought his soul down to quivering, with small shame.
And he was fit to run, if his chance had come.
But Gloucesters of more sterner frame and spirit
Kept him in place without reproach, (sweet blood inherit
From hills, and nature) said no word and kept him there.
True, he'd have fought to death, but Laventie's needing
Was a nerve to hide the pain of the soul bleeding –
Say nothing, and nothing ever of God to beg.
He hurt more, did fatigues, and was friend to share
What food was not his need; of enemies not heeding.
Everybody was glad – (but determined to hide the bad)
When he took courage at wiremending and shot his leg,
And got to Blighty, no man saying word of denying.

Leaving a soft job

Detached men, hearing our Infantry were about to move,
Not satisfied with our comfort or our safety (in proof)
The desire also stirred us to see company, our Battallions,
Greet comrades again, and freeze with them in the cut rough
Ditches of Picardy, Artois or of La Flandre
True, we were warm of nights, and heard not the violence
Of shells threatening imminent death on our dug-out's roof;
Hunger, and love-longing and of soldiership so commander,
We would bear no more our quiet, but made applications
To return to our regiments loved, whatever might be the chance.
Warwicks, Berks, Worcesters, or old honoured Gloucesters.
Because honour is honour, this comfort is not enough;
Not enough for the shame of safety without blame.
What though the lovely Ancre made marsh of lucent wonder
At sunset gloom, what though freedom were remembered once
Clearer here, than with burnishing of straps and buttons?
The fame of colours, the glory of old battles called 'ours' there
And Crucifix Corner it seemed better (a little) to leave,
Though afterwards we for candles and such warmth might grieve
Hoping a march at least with war-loved companions.
And in (at least) goodness of hardship again to believe.

Chaulnes

They retreated, we passed there, through most dreadful tangles of wire
(Impregnable it seemed with any of Infantry fire.)
Passed the damned Pillboxes, concrete places, wonder how Fritz
Could give up such a position; and all in bits
Everything was; knocked flat by such devil-of-evil war
As for near three years had hurt Artois, Picardy, with mortal hurt.
Later, we found our comrade's grave, they had buried him
(Found his body, loved his face, carefully had carried him,
                              tended him.)
And heard the words of commemoration said ceremonious over
The white cross and the little mound; Europe even now had care
Of Europe; this great spirit killed in the reckless night;
Buried with danger's tenderness by his loving enemies.
The Gloucesters watching the cross, craftsman's work, past their loss
Remembered gratitude, and praised chivalry for this
True-burial of a comrade loved best of all the companies.
Honoured the care had fashioned so honourable a cross.
And forgot our grief, but not hunger in noble billets
Of Omiecourt, where much wood was, and there I found many
                              postcards
Of German towns nailed up for memory's rewards,
Two great books of plainsong in noble print with the wets
And dirts of perhaps two Winters blotting notes and words.
Hunger and fatigue, clear county after the wires and the bullets.

The Curses

Curses on packs that weigh a ton too heavy!
(Comrade you carry books; one sticks out, believe me!)
Curses on marching cobbles the left hand man.
(True, one needs his legs unequal, a difficult plan.)
Curses on halts that disappear like mere seconds.
(You should take your watch out, measure it all – each tick, reckoned.)
Curses on shoulders that will not settle to steady
To bear the weight of equipment, the spirit ready.
(Yes, but when you have parcels, and there's half of a cake
In your haversack, and Cobbett, Borrow and William Shake-
speare in your left pack, in your right Walt Whitman;
Spirit of Man – an anthology, and a bit, man,
Of that remarkable author William Wordsworth.
In your trenching tool cover, Keats, yet the child of earth.
A chess set hidden somewhere, and the Everyman *Century
of Essays* stuffed in your tunic out of harm's way.
Really, really, you must fill your head with your learning,
Until no more the blisters on your feet are burning.
Abstract your consciousness till the pack weighs a jolly sight less
Than light fatigue in Mayfair, less than evening dress.
Buck up, lad, if libraries move, even Carnegie
Would admit it were better to bribe some odd kind A.S.C.
Lorry to move your knowledge, than to march the one only
Scholar – in glory and misery, Noble and lonely.)
Reflecting he had been a signaller in happier times,
When occasionally he might scribble or study rhymes –
The loaded one burst out into the last of his curses,
"Curses on them who scorn a private's reverses.
And will not show sympathy, but play chess with dreadful cunning,
While he may not blow clear even his nose that's running,
Nor read the things that weigh to bother old sweats or horses."

War Books

What did they expect of our toil and extreme
Hunger – the perfect drawing of a heart's dream?
Did they look for a book of wrought art's perfection,
Who promised no reading, nor praise, nor publication?
Out of the heart's sickness the spirit wrote
For delight, or to escape hunger, or of war's worst anger,
When the guns died to silence and men would gather sense
Somehow together, and find this was life indeed,
And praise another's nobleness, or to Cotswold get hence;
There we wrote – Corbie Ridge – or in Gonnehem at rest -
Or Fauquissart – our world's death songs, ever the best.
One made sorrows' praise passing the church where silence
Opened for the long quivering strokes of the bell –
Another wrote all soldiers' praise, and of France and night's stars,
Served his guns, got immortality, and died well.
But Ypres played another trick with its danger on me,
Kept still the needing and loving-of-action body,
Gave no candles, and nearly killed me twice as well,
And no souvenirs, though I risked my life in the stuck tanks.
Yet there was praise of Ypres, love came sweet in hospital,
And old Flanders went under to long ages of plough thought in my
pages.

Further Reading

Editions

Collected Poems ed. P. J. Kavanagh (OUP, 1982).

Severn & Somme and War's Embers ed. R. K. R. Thornton (MidNAG/ Carcanet, 1987; pbk 1997).

Selected Poems ed. P. J. Kavanagh (OUP, 1990).

Best Poems and the Book of Five Makings ed. R. K. R. Thornton (MidNAG/ Carcanet, 1995),

Ivor Gurney, Everyman's Poetry, ed. George Walter (J. M. Dent, 1996)

Rewards of Wonder ed. George Walter (MidNAG/Carcanet, 2000)

80 Poems or So ed. George Walter and R. K. R. Thornton (MidNAG/ Carcanet 2002).

Jon Stallworthy, *Three Poets of the First World War* (Penguin, 2011).

A three-volume edition of all of Gurney's poems is being prepared by Philip Lancaster and Tim Kendall to be published by OUP, which will gather together all the poems, of which many are unpublished.

Biography and Letters

The Ordeal of Ivor Gurney by Michael Hurd (OUP, 1978)

Ivor Gurney: War Letters ed. R. K. R. Thornton (MidNAG/Carcanet, 1983)

Collected Letters of Ivor Gurney ed. R. K. R. Thornton (MidNAG/Carcanet, 1991).

Ivor Gurney and Marion Scott: Song of Pain and Beauty by Pamela Blevins (Boydell Press, 2008).

Ivor Gurney: Dweller in Shadows, a biography by Kate Kennedy, is in preparation.

Criticism

John Lucas, *Ivor Gurney,* Writers and their Work (Northcote House, 2001)

Tim Kendall, *Modern English War Poetry* (OUP, 2006). Chapter 5.

Eleanor Rawling, *Ivor Gurney's Gloucestershire: Exploring Poetry and Place* (History Press, 2011)

Continuing critical work on Gurney both as poet and musician is printed in the *Ivor Gurney Society Journal,* which will shortly reach its twentieth edition.

Selected Discography

Severn Meadows: Songs by Ivor Gurney. Hyperion CDA67243 (2001). Paul Agnew (*tenor*); Julius Drake (*piano*).

Ivor Gurney – Songs: Naxos 8.572151 (2009). Susan Bickley (*mezzo-soprano*); Iain Burnside (*piano*).

War's Embers: Songs by Browne, Butterworth, Farrar, Gurney, Kelly. Hyperion CDA66261/2 (1997). Michael George (*baritone*); Martyn Hill (*tenor*); Stephen Varcoe (*baritone*); Clifford Benson (*piano*).

Severn and Somme: Songs by Gurney, Howells, Sanders, Wilson, Venables. SOMM CD057 (2006). Roderick Williams (*baritone*); Susie Allan (*piano*).

The Dark Pastoral: Songs and Poetry from World War One. Altara ALT1035 (2008). Andrew Kennedy (*tenor*); Julius Drake (*piano*)

Ludlow and Teme: Song cycle for tenor, string quartet and piano Signum SIGD112 (2008). Andrew Kennedy (*tenor*); Simon Crawford-Phillips (*piano*); Dante String Quartet.

Lights Out: Song cycle (orchestrated by Jeremy Dibble) Dutton CDLX7243 (2010). Roderick Williams (*baritone*); BBC Concert Orchestra, conducted by Martin Yates.

War Elegy: BBC Symphony Orchestra, conductor David Lloyd-Jones Dutton CDLX7171 (2006).

Violin Sonata in E Flat Major: Rupert Marshall-Luck (*violin*); Matthew Rickard (*piano*). EM Records CD011(2012).

For more information check the Society's website at www.ivorgurney.org.uk/

The Secretary of the Ivor Gurney Society is
Philip Richardson,
44 Fir Tree Avenue,
Wallingford,
Oxfordshire OX10 0PD
UK
panderichardson@btinternet.com